I AM

(Reflections of a Spiritual Rebirth)

John St Julien

I do not ask you to believe anything in these words.
I point only to a guiding light of great love that can awaken in us all.
May the voice and presence of that light awaken in you,
and may the world know its love through all you are.

John St Julien

I dedicate this book to the children of Feathers Tale Children's Village and Angels Gate Home for street-involved children. I also dedicate it to the protectors of unconditional love and presence in our family, the rescue dogs. This family we started has grown to nearly two hundred children and over one hundred dogs who needed a loving home. The message of this book is one of hope, to guide my fellow man to the space in our consciousness where a voice not of this world resides. That voice led me to start this family, and now I burn with a passion for seeing others trust that voice, follow that voice, and see its love manifest in the world around me—just as that great love, its presence, its will, and its guidance made manifest this family and the structure by which we make that family possible. www.sharetanzania.com

A thank you to Alecia Shepherd for designing the front cover,
after the passing of my beloved dog Assissi.

ISBN: 979-8367298949

Introduction

*L*ike you, I happened to be born here on Earth, manifest as a conscious being, a being with a propensity for love, hatred, joy, anguish, happiness, sorrow, peace, anger, pleasure, and discomfort.

I, like you, was born into a species and a system that does not really understand where we are. We are on a planet floating in a void of apparent nothingness called space. It seems easy to accept, but in reality, out of fear, we use these terms and words to feel safe and secure and provide a sense we understand it; we get it. We really don't, though. Science cannot explain where we go when we die or if we go at all. In short, science cannot explain why we are here, how we are here, or what here is.

As a fellow human, I would often ask a question when younger: "After so many generations of humans walking this Earth, why have we not come to a unified consensus on how to best be a human—a guidebook, an instruction manual?" It seems to make sense, undoubtedly; we have guidebooks on how to write, pray, cook, exercise, paint, start a business, and even find God. Yet there is no instruction manual on what it is to be a human and how to best be happy and walk that path.

After years of self-exploration, I discovered something quite startling. Placing analysis and thought first is only sometimes the best road to take as a human. Beyond that, I found that our society had taught me very clearly who I was—that I was John, an Englishman with (x) qualifications; but that, in fact, I wasn't. Nor are you your name, your nationality, or your academic achievements. You are something far more significant and expansive than that, and I aim to show you this with this book.

Some of you will know who I am and what I have done. Still, for those who do not, I must share something fundamental about the life I've lived. The discoveries I, as many, have awakened into the awareness of.

I discovered who I truly was, and when I did, I chose to live my life without thought and analysis at the forefront. Instead, I decided to connect to something far more intelligent than my mind. That was the very force that made you grow from child to man or woman, the force that is growing your hair and beating your heart. When I did, while living a life like most in the western world, I received communication from that intelligence. It asked me to go to Tanzania, a specific village even.

I knew nothing about Tanzania, Africa, or travel. I had never left Europe, in fact. Yet I was so sure that this voice beyond self and analysis had spoken, that I followed it. I was not rich by any measure; I had a few thousand pounds in the bank. This is important, as your analysis self will happily account this to wealth, but that's not true. After six months, I was totally broke in Tanzania, with literally not even enough to sustain myself.

I, however, knew this intelligence that led me there, one of great compassion, had a plan. No idea what the plan was; I just knew.

Now, I have a Facebook and YouTube channel, and that plan was revealed. I started a family out there, but none of the children are biologically my own. That family has grown to nearly two hundred children, all of which were living in crisis and had no one to care for them, half of which had special needs. We have over one hundred rescue dogs these days; I can't forget the pack. Beyond there, we have provided education to thousands of children struggling in poverty and child labor. You may wonder how big your house must be to house two hundred children and more than one hundred dogs. By the direction of that unseen force of great love, we built a village from scratch to provide a loving home for all those beautiful beings I am blessed to call family.

What I discovered as a human was life-changing. I entered a space in awareness and consciousness that completely changed how I interacted with reality, lived my life, and moved through this world. This is a space where our true nature is restored, and we realize that our true nature, that true power of the human being, quite seemingly, was not lost by chance.

Your life is too short to not ask who you are at least once. I hope you stay with me to discover what it means to be a human, with traits that appear almost supernatural to our mainstream state of awareness.

Chapter 1: Who Exactly Are You?

(Beyond Words)

If you are reading this, there is a good chance that you have stumbled into a particular set of questions, as I once did.

"Who am I?"

"What is this all about?"

"Surely there is more to life than this?"

"Why aren't I happy?"

"What is the meaning of my life?"

"Is there a God?"

"Where do I go when I die?"

"Where did they go when they died?"

"Am I enough?"

"If I had done that differently, where would I be?"

And on and on and on . . .

For some, these questions come and go; for others, however, they inspire a quest—a mission to find answers, to find out the truth, and to peer somehow into the mysteries of life that countless others have and countless more will. Perhaps that quest has led you to this book. If it has, I will ask you a question that set this human typing here on a path to the means to find answers to all that was listed and more.

"Who is the one asking questions here?"

If I were to ask you that, you might say as I did, "Well, it's me, ———." On the face of it this is a very valid answer. For all of your life, those around you have pointed at you, this walking, talking expression of humanity. An expression shaped in the form of the one reading this, with the word of your name, "John" in my instance. Your name usually comes at the beginning of a long list of answers to such question as, "Who are you?" and "Who is the one asking all the questions here?"

"I am John. I am an Englishman. I am human. I am a father, a husband, a brother, a son, a grandson. I am the founder of a charity. I am a YouTube spiritual guide. I am a Christian, a . . ." and the list goes on and on and on.

Yet let us look at this list together for a moment. However, to look at it clearly, we need to become untangled from all these labels and roles in life. They are pretty complicated for many of us and filled with many emotive memories and senses of self we are proud of, love or hate, or indeed are ashamed of.

So let me ask you this, are you aware that you are your name? Yes, of course you are. Are you aware you are your nationality? Yes, of course you are. Are you aware you are someone's child or perhaps someone's parent? Of course you are.

Are you aware of the label of your career just now in life? Doctor, bus driver, teacher, entrepreneur? Yes, indeed you are.

So, if you are sitting there wondering what my point is, it is this: The point is that if you know your name, nationality, and relationship labels, your academic or career labels, then who is the one who is aware of those labels?

Who is that? If you are aware of all these roles and labels in life that have been placed upon you, then who is the awareness that is aware of them?

You were aware as a child that you were a student in a particular school. You are aware, or may someday be aware, that you are a parent, maybe a grandparent. Perhaps you will be aware of a great deal as you play out your role in this dance of the human story we are all in, but who is the awareness that is aware of these ever-changing roles in life?

Let us look at emotions, something we all must learn to navigate here as humans. When you are happy, you are aware that you are happy. When you are sad, you are aware that you are sad. Is the awareness happy and sad? Or is that still just this unnamed awareness that was silently aware throughout the endless, often chaotic, and sometimes peaceful changes we all walk through here on this Earth.

It is within the ability of humankind, which you are also aware you are part of, to examine such essential questions. For all I have lived, life seems reliant on us knowing who we are and are not.

All these roles, names, nationalities, relationships, academic achievements, etc. can all be placed under one label to help us continue this communication together more efficiently. I will call that collection of roles and memories of who we are "self" from now on. When I refer to self, I am referring to the roles and labels we place on our lives, not the awareness beneath it all.

Now, if I have done my job well, we should have a grasp of the difference between awarenss and self. For many, this may be a revelation to know that beneath the constant mental noise that makes up the self, there is the awareness.

This leads me to my next point: Self is made up of thought; that is, thought is the material on which self is built.

Awareness is aware of thought, but unlike self, it is not made up of thoughts. Awareness is made up of something entirely different, and we will get into that later.

So, the self is made up of thoughts, which you are aware of, and since you are aware of your thoughts, you surely are not your thoughts. You are the one who is aware of the thoughts. Therefore, you are not the self, you are the awareness.

I hope we have established this and that you are sitting with it comfortably. We have established that you are aware of the self you have been walking around believing yourself to be. Next, we really need to unravel who this awareness is, and then connect with it. Exploring these questions from awareness is an intensely joyous and peaceful endeavour. Exploring from the self, however, is often quite the opposite, as you may have experienced.

First question, when did we lose track of awareness and become tangled in self?

Let us all imagine back to our infancy. If I were to lay you down as a baby next to a tree seedling and place a time-lapse camera above you, comparing you as an infant to the tree as a seedling, growing beside one another, then what would we see? We would see the tree seedling taking its nourishment from the sun, rain, and soil; whereas with you, we would see a child needing its nutrition from mum, who is taking her energy from plants that, like the tree, take it from the sun, rain, and soil.

If we watched the timelapse, the baby you and the tree seedling both would grow from that source of nourishment. You would not know exactly how you were growing up, nor would your parents. You would all just be aware that you are growing, and would be aware of the tree seedling growing as well.

Now, both the seedling and the baby continue to grow, and we watch as they silently grow. And we ask "Who is growing them? Who is the intelligence growing the tree, and who is the intelligence growing the child?" It is clearly not the self. The self is barely formed, and you are, at the same time, aware that this growth is taking place. Even now, you know your hair is growing, albeit slowly, but you know it is. How are you doing that?

We watch the baby and tree grow silently together. We add no labels to either, and we see that they grow as long as nourishment is available. That silent growth continues, the seedling into a tree continues, and the baby into a child, adolescent, and so on, continues. We are still watching this timelapse, but now we can ask, what are we watching a timelapse of?

Imagine If I had placed next to the tree seedling a petri dish of fungi, and the pair, seedling and fungi, were growing side by side on our silent timelapse. What would you sense you are watching? Nature? The natural course of life and mother nature?

Did you feel that way when a baby was there, a baby you? When you look back at yourself as a baby, as a child, as you have aged even . . . do you ever see the source of your growth as nature? Go outside and listen to a tree grow for a moment. Just listen to it. Watch it. Listen. You know it is growing, but try to listen to it grow. Now look at one of your fingernails and do the same. Listen to it grow. It is growing, and you don't have any say in it. So listen to it growing. No scientific labels. Listen only, and you might just hear the one growing it as you listen, but more on that later.

So here is the problem, you, like all of us, might say, "I love being in nature." But from what I have said here, I hope you can see you *are* nature. What on Earth has made you feel separated from it? This is a question we should be asking.

Suddenly, this manifestation of nature is shaped as the "you"—the infant is given a label, a sound commonly known as a "name," the sound that other humans use to point at this manifestation in and of nature that you are.

You take this name, and when you hear it, you respond. Great, practical, and very useful in fact. However, what's next? Brothers and sisters, likes and dislikes, school and chores, etc. Slowly but surely, you begin to store all these things as memories. If you are taught by wise parents, they will teach you memory control, but I know not one person raised by such parents in our time. The result is memories that are brought forth into every element of the mind. Not only to recall past lessons to function well in the now, but also to build an image of who you are in your thoughts. These memories, in turn, take up space in the brain, and in fact, they can stop the brain from interacting with the now.

So now, if we can imagine the timelapse again, we see the child is growing, and the tree also. Both are growing, but we have one storing labels and roles—the combination of memory and thought. Initially, growing as pure awareness, experiencing the growth, hunger, and joy of the human story. Then, you have thoughts and memories inserted into that growth. The tree does not have that blessing; the tree just is.

However, how long before the gift of thought and memory become a curse? By curse, I mean that which leads the child to stop realizing its unity with intelligence beyond the self, an intelligence that planeted planets, forested forests, and humaned humans.

The answer lies in what I am doing here right now: I am using words. You see, with words we lose track of reality pretty quickly.

Both this writer and you the reader do it daily, I guarantee you. You go outside, and you see the beautiful sky. "Sky," what is that? This big blue wonder above us. Yet most never look at it with a sense of "What on earth is this, what is this place, this mystery we live under . . .?" Rather, we just see the word "sky" and move on. I will elaborate on this more shortly, but for now, even the word "sky" in this example creates a false understanding. Well, I know what it is; it's the sky. What is the sky, though? You can take scientific language and say a great deal, or take spiritual language and say a great deal. Still, in the end, neither the scientists nor the spiritualists have idea what it is.

Every word they use to define "sky" leads to the same road: oxygen, ozone . . .what is that? It's a molecule or collection of molecules. What is a molecule? It's made up of atoms and electrons. What are atoms and electrons? As far as we see, they are the material that all things are made of. Are you 100 percent confident of this? No, we can't be, as the behaviour of ions, etc., alter with observation. Atoms are made up mainly of space. What is space? We don't know . . . and so, the word "sky" is a cover for the uncomfortable truth that you, I, we—every one with our shared analytical mind, and all its labels—don't know.

Here I hope it is seen that words can kill the moment and, with it, our actual depth of interaction, connection, and place in it. The truth is that moment I mention, to most, is lost under a blanket of words. It is where we live, but finding it with the ways and perceptions we are raised by within western society is actually impossible.

That moment and how we live in it is a profoundly valuable space. We did not live yesterday, and we will not live tomorrow. For if I built you a time machine, and then I asked you to go forwards in time to tomorrow, you would arrive, but upon stepping out of the machine, to you and your senses functioning in reality, it would be here and now in the moment again.

You would get into the machine here and now, and some dials

and the setting would change. You would disembark from your conscious state of functioning in reality, from your individual point of awareness, here and now. However, to your awareness, whether you went forwards or backwards in time, every time you stepped out of that machine, you would be in the here and now. As you travelled through this notion of time, you would be here and now, watching that happen.

Words take us from that here and now, for the structure of the self is set deeply in endless words. I can sit here, now, fully present. I hear the birds calling, leaves moving in the wind, my computer gently humming, and my children playing in the background. It's beautiful to take in. As I describe each passing sound and sight arriving with the human writing this, I move the awareness away from it. I do so as words are linear, filled with time. Awareness of the moment, this silent timelapse of birth to death we are all in, doesn't need time or words. We only need words to communicate to one another, to point at what we see, hear, feel, taste, and smell here and now.

So as a child growing up, you were not taught how words mask both dull and intense terms. Then, in no time at all, your words will kill the moment.

We begin to see the words and not reality. We see the word "tree" and not this bizarre is-ness of life. We say it's made of wood, and it's undoubtedly not just that. A tree is much more. When seen without a label, it is an arising of such mystery, such beauty, such sacredness. Yet we see this sacredness, and we say "tree." And if that label remains, the connection to its majesty, its sacred nature, is lost.

This is what we are doing to the baby, also. Even if the baby is us, we see the words we have covered it with. Seeing these words, this is not his or her or our majesty. It is not our wonder, our rarity, magic, freedom, and sacredness. Our wonderment is lost, for it is not seen in words. It is seen first without words, then language points us to it again.

Therefore, we are beyond words. This leaves me with the tremendously difficult task of using words to point at what we are in

13

such a manner that you, the reader, do not get lost in these words. Instead, may you find yourself pointed towards becoming lost in that which they are pointing towards.

Suppose I have succeeded with this chapter in creating a line, a space between self and awareness. Having done so, I hope this book will go fine from here on; but if I have not, then come back to this and ask yourself, "Who is aware?" Try not to over-analyse; just ask it until you find the undeniable truth. You are aware of all the roles of self, and therefore, you know you can't be self. You are not thoughts and memories. You are more. And I hope, in some greatly increasing way, aware you are more.

"Wait though," you say, "I love being a [mother, a father, a son], a [doctor, a taxi driver]." That's great; that's wonderful. I also love being a father and son, husband and charity founder. What I don't love, however, is the suffering of forgetting I am more. The battle for peace and joy arises in me when I get lost in the roles and distanced from the space in which I am aware I am these things. I don't love losing track of the intelligence beating my heart, playing a role in how well I parent my sons or how I am with building villages for children in crisis.

This is the point, you see. It is not to say goodbye to self. It is to put the self in its correct spot and let the untapped potential revive that self with new intelligence, vigour, love, and compassion. Let the self in all its ways be, but stop letting it drive you into one problem and worry after another problem and worry. Instead, see if awareness can drive life for a time, and give self the break it has earned, and you need.

Chapter 2: What Is This Awareness?

(Pure Life Energy)

*J*f I have succeeded in the first chapter, then you have found a space whereby you have become aware of both self and awareness.

Now the question is, what is this awareness?

As you've discovered, self is made up of thoughts, words, and memories. Our attention gets lost in these quite often. All have such an essential and profound value. It is beyond precious to call our children by their names, to ground ourselves into lives, to function with one another. The mind helps us to recognize those we have shared much with in our passage of time here. Memory should be used to recall past events and to make the moment you are in go more smoothly, but most don't use memory that way.

This self is truly an incredible thing and a blessing to us all in the right circumstances. When that self, however, becomes intolerable—as we see in society with the tremendous suicide rates, addiction rates, and more—that self really can become the polar opposite of a blessing to many of our fellow humans. I know, for I was once one such human, who simply could not live with the self my mind had conjured up and clung to.

What provided me with escape was awareness, and beyond awareness, recognizing what awareness was, what it connects us to, and the truth, peace, and love it provides us.

Before I jump in and boldly state what awareness is, I will share something else with you, that is we must get out of the habit of wanting people to tell us how it is and agreeing or disagreeing. This is how the self likes it, but this leaves room for error. You may agree or disagree with someone who has it totally wrong. Or you may be left wondering if you are confident, as belief is not a certainty. Sadly, this way of living has meant that as a man falls—which we can, do, and will—then any truth he may have represented to a believer may have become discredited. If a man, however, leads you to see the truth, then he falls, you can separate the two with ease and acknowledge he is human. The truth he showed you is a fact you are grateful to have been led towards before he fell.

So, it is best to see it yourself, not to agree or disagree. I hope to point you to that space, the space where you do not need the guidance of another human. The guidance, which is the light that illuminates your path, will come directly from the intelligence that is shining the sun and beating your heart. It is the same intelligence that knit you together in your mother's womb, an intelligence that clearly knows what it is doing, or you wouldn't be here.

Let us attempt to discover, together, this awareness that you are. This awareness is aware of all the roles, names, labels, memories, and relationships you have said you are. Yet it is somehow beyond entanglement in them.

Let us make a little space in ourselves. If we come at this with too much self and not enough intelligence, too much knowledge and not enough intuition and heart, we will pollute our clarity of seeing.

Hanging Your Tags on a Tree

So, to make some space, I invite you into a quiet forest far from the bustle of life. As we enter, there is a beautiful tree where I will ask you to hang up everything you don't need. We will do this so that we can clearly see and inquire as to what this awareness is.

Start with your name; you don't need it now, so hang it on the tree. Age next, let's hang that up. It's not essential for now. You can grab both of them on the way out of the forest. Nationality, you have had that from birth, but you don't need that now. Let's just put it on this tree for a moment.

Already you are becoming lighter and our vision less clouded, I hope. Next, hang up relationships on the tree: son, brother, husband, father; daughter, sister, wife, mother; friend, grandparent, etc.—whatever you may be. I know these are particularly hard to hang up, but it's only for a brief time. Let us put them on this tree together. Next up, academic labels, work titles, career path, etc. These will not assist us in inquiring about this awareness. They go on the tree.

Next, let us place our spiritual practices and self-labels on this tree, only for a time; those structures are not needed now. Next, your religious identity goes on the tree, just for a moment. It is not that you are turning away from it, not at all. if anything, we will be drawing closer to it, but afterward. Just hang it on this tree while we as humans inquire who this awareness that is aware of our religious belief and identity. Next, our scientific labels must also be hung up: human, man, woman; we don't need those for now.Next, we will take memory and hang it there on the tree. All these other items on the tree were relying on memory in their own way.

We have hung much of all we are in this world on this tree. There is likely more to go with it. However, before we proceed into this forest to find out who this awareness is, let's say a stranger walks by and sees what we are doing. He asks you a question as he looks at the tree and all that is hanging there. "Who is the one hanging things on that tree?" he asks.

You may feel compelled to say, "Well, it's me." But right now, you know it's not. You have hung your name on the tree.

"Well, it's me, a human," you might start to say, but you just put those scientific labels on the tree as well. Since you put them on the tree, they really can't be you, can they? If they were you, then you would not have been able to put them there.

"It's me, the son of ——," oh no, that's a relationship, and it's hanging on the tree. You could have said, "It is me, a Christian," but no, that's on the tree also.

Eventually, if you go deep down into this, you will see you are left with limited answers to the inquiry,

"Who is hanging all those things on the tree?"

Answer one: "I don't know."

Okay, good, hold onto that thought.

Answer two: "Me." But who is me? You no longer know, as all the terms you would use to describe yourself are on the tree.

So, the only answer to "Who is me?" is: "I don't know . . ."

Hold onto that.

Answer three: "I am. I am the one hanging all those things on the tree."

"I am . . ."

"I am. I am. I am."

But who is "I am" then?

"I don't know," you say, and so this begins opening the doorway into truth that most humans are struggling to open.

"I am hanging all those things on the tree." This sentence does not lack significance, not if you look at it. You are brought back to the bare bones of yourself here. You have returned to the point of immense innocence, like a child even. This might be a good thing, for Jesus said, "Unless you become as children, you may not enter the kingdom."

You have no definitions, labels, or pretenses of what you are, where you are, and why you are. You have stopped pretending you understand this mystery as you were taught. Your words and labels have stopped, the structure of self you have used your whole life has stopped, and yet you are still here, doing, seeing, and hanging things on the tree.

Without the self that you have hung up, you are left with this state of not knowing. You can only say, "I am" or "I don't know." They both point to the same truth. Despite not knowing, you are nevertheless still here and still doing and seeing. You are still aware. If moved into correctly—and if the self does not, in its discomfort, jump in to try and analyse and control it again—then it is a state of humility, of innocence, of virgin consciousness that remains. For what is more humble than a man or woman with no self to interfere in life's unfoldment?

Awareness, the I am, is pure life energy looking through a body you once thought was owned by your name, your nationality, and your roles. Without self, how can one human feel more than another human? You recognize the "I am" that you are is actually the "I am" that other humans are also.

Most have gotten lost in the labels, but they don't see it. They believe the self is who they are, and that they are the self who is hanging these labels on the tree. With no self, you are no longer analysing life, yet you are still in it, part of it.

Once you understand this, you have become free of anything between your interaction with the world and the cosmic intelligence that is growing your hair even as you read this.

In the Bible, it states, "God guides the humble . . ." (Psalm 25:9). Is this humility the empty state? Is this the state where the saints found the presence of this loving force that led them to great deeds of compassion that they pointed at with the word God?

Through investigating awareness, we have reached a space of the I am. We have reached the sense of childlike humility.

All of your attempts at building a self to make sense of this life are hung on the tree, yet as you have discovered, someone is still here, and that someone is aware they have hung those labels on the tree.

You have stripped away religious imagery and spiritual and scientific definitions, and yet you have continued to be. Beyond this, the only way you could possibly verbalize who is hanging these things on the tree is by saying, in astonishing innocence as you look at all these labels and roles hanging there, either "I am" or "I don't know," which in essence is the same answer, for this "I am" state, as I will call it, seems equivalent to admitting, "I don't know." The analytical mind will try to know, but in vain. If it digs deep enough, it will reach the truth of the "I am," which is a state of "I don't know, yet here I am."

In the Bible, God gave the answer only once, in Exodus 3:14, when asked for his name he said, "I am that I am."

Jesus was asked about his authority, and he also responded with, "I am."

*T*ruly, truly, I say to you, before Abraham was, I am.
(John 8:58, ESV)

Now I am not saying I am God. I do not know how my liver works as it does or what my body does when I sleep. I can not make these body systems function. I am saying that this state of deduction of self and all its labels—this backward engineering to the space of "I am" or "I don't know" is a space in consciousness where a profound love has overtaken many a man, and a deeply profound and positive transformation has occurred with it.

We should define this, however, as I remind you that words do not equate to reality. Your mind might be throwing up images and opinions of God that are not the images my mind holds. It may be throwing up judgments, hurts, rebellious memories, and ideas that God is terrible and a dated concept. It may be throwing up images of a man in the sky who wants your money. Or your mind may have images of a God who has created immense suffering in the world, through wars and inquisitions. You'd be right, for the image of God in man's mind has done all those things, no doubt about it; whereas others who have known God's presence speak of great love, compassion, intelligence, and wisdom guiding their lives.—just as Jesus spoke of and lived for in his teachings.

Somehow there is one set of humans that act as monsters, lacking love and compassion, and do so in the name of God, while the other set are saints, who are filled with empathy and selfless acts of love. Suppose you have truly separated from self in some way. In that case, I want to pose this to you: maybe, just maybe, it is because one set knew only of God in the realm of self—self and all its words, labels, and images—and the other set, the saints, knew God without the self. That other set has known God through the space of the I am. The awareness, the I am, lacks analysis. Instead of coming from a place of classification and segmentation, it comes from a place of unification. This state of allowing, of letting go, can be loosely defined with the word "surrender."

Meister Eckhart wrote, "Nothing in all creation is so like God as stillness." I would add: Nothing is as still as a human who has hit the sleep button on self, which is to hit the sleep button on thought, analysis, and memory for a time.

Where then do awareness and God meet? After all, we are here to ask who or what this awareness is, not who or what God is.

After chapter one, I hope there is a clear realization that we are aware of the self, so the self is not us, for we are aware of it.

We have then inquired here into awareness. Reaching for a space of freedom to inquire, we have deduced a position where our only response for who this one looking out of the body is must be either "I am" or "I don't know." Yet here we are, still here seeing, hearing, touching, etc. When we hang on the tree that which makes up self—labels, thoughts, stories, memories—then we just are.

Science has added endless labels to try and deduce what you are and where you are. Spirituality, religion, and philosophy have done the same. Yet they have built all of what we call reality on a foundation of the unknown. If they had known, they would never have started trying to explain in the first place. We have reached the space where awareness, the I am doer that is awareness stripped back to virgin consciousness, is unknown and seems unknowable.

Recognizing the tremendous unknown you are and are of, and in some peculiar way is what you are, is an acknowledgment of immense unity. You have come to an understanding that when you put the labels of the self on the tree, then what is left to call "you" is awareness, the I am, the unknown. The self is all a game of the mind, a needed one, but one that is lethal if it drowns out the I am-ness within, for when it does, it drowns out the unity.

The analytical mind categorizes and separates. The awareness has no differentiation. It is unity, immense love. There compassion for one another is born. You love not because you should, or because God told you to love one another, but because you simply, inescapably do. So, awareness is the great unknown, and when we inquire into awareness, we reach the I am. I don't know, yet I am still here, still doing, still existing. This sounds like a dead end, but it's not. This is the beginning of the love, peace, and truth you have likely heard taught by Jesus Christ.

Awareness is the doorway to union with all things, the union with the I am that was here from the beginning, the Word, the I am that you have begun to see is looking out from you. It exists even without the mind's structures to define and ground it.

If we can find the I am, we can find humility. If we can find humility, we can find unity. If we can find unity, we will know love, great love. Somehow awareness leads us to this blank canvas in us, our virgin consciousness. Once we have found that, might we be able to give birth to such qualities in our actions and intelligence that Jesus represented?

Chapter 3: Then, Where Are You?

(A Mystery)

*T*his will be a short chapter. For some of you, the last chapters might have already answered the question of "Where are you?"

You and I, and all of humanity, have defined ourselves based on language and reference, including having defined your location.

"I am John. I am in Europe. I am on planet Earth. Planet Earth is in a solar system. That solar system is in a galaxy. That galaxy is in a universe. That universe is potentially in a multiverse. That multiverse is in . . . ?" Eventually, you run out of a point of reference, you see? It always happens with everything you say if you investigate it thoroughly.

Awareness allows us to break from the character we have built around this language and these references. And when we do, that character is still here, this awareness that we are is still here, still doing, seeing, hearing—only now the image of self is not organizing it. We realize that we just took a break from a hugely complex game of make-believe. One that gives the self immense comfort. It was sturdy and happy in its illusion of knowing. The self is glad to live life knowing it is in Europe, on earth, and in space. Yet this game of language and reference ends in the reality that you have no idea where you are. Your only reference for where you are is based on language, which is based on reference. Run out of references, and you reach the wonderful truth, the liberating truth: You do not know where you are. You do not know what you are, how you are, and why you are. Yet still, you are here.

We have some understanding of our reality through science. We know that it is based on vibration and materials we call atoms that vibrate differently based on the form they make in what we perceive as matter. We know this as science. Biblically, a word is a vibration of atoms arriving at your eardrums, so this matches up, albeit with very different linguistic frameworks.

*I*n the beginning was the Word, and the Word was with God, and the Word was God. (John 1:1)

Yet deep down, for all our analysis and efforts, no one on earth knows where we are, for in time, they run out of references to locate things like the universe and multiverse . . . So, then what? Something we don't have a name for, that we don't know. Yet, language is not reality. These words are masking the inescapable truth of the great unknown, the great mystery that we are. The more we see this mystery, the less we need self—thought, analysis, etc. The more time we spend in that mystery, in fact, the more sensible faith begins to seem. I will need to define faith, and I will do so in the following chapter, but for now, just accept it. First we must define what we are following in this space of I am, the surrendered, loving witness. this awareness state we have begun to peer into.

You will see that the whole notion of where you are is built on words that use other words as a reference. In time, you will run out of references, and finally you will have to admit it is a mystery where we are, which is a good thing. That is an important thing, for that leaves us with two options. For one, we could analyze every endless fragment of existence until we know. Alternatively, we could try something different: we could try unifying with it, to see if spending time there allows us to know. For, after all, "we walk by faith, not by sight (2 Cor. 5:7)."

Chapter 4: What Is Spiritual Rebirth?

(Spirit Man)

I named this book "I Am: Reflections of Spiritual Rebirth," yet I have not mentioned spiritual rebirth until now, the fourth chapter. Nonetheless, you have made it this far, and hopefully the foundations of the first chapters have created some freedom from self. For self is the home of human arrogance and pride, the element in all of mankind that conditions love and rejects the effortless compassion born of unity with it.

So, what is spiritual rebirth? It has had many names and terms, it seems. To be "born again" is a very familiar term in the west due to Christianity. Is perhaps "enlightenment" the same thing? "Spiritual awakening" also? What about the term "Ascension"?

In our human story just now, spiritual rebirth is attached to the teachings of Jesus, who spoke of it while engaging in conversation with Nicodemus, a Pharisee, a religious man, one seeking the mystic truths of Spirit and of love. But he was not after thoughts and ideas of that love, as many are caught up in today. Rather he sought transformation. Imagine being transformed into a human so overrun by love that you must love, for you feel consumed by its presence. In John 3:3–8, the Bible states it thusly,

Jesus answered him, "Truly, truly, I say to you, unless one

is born again he cannot see the kingdom of God." [4]Nicode-mus said to him, "How can a man be born when he is old? Can he enter a second time into his mother's womb and be born?" [5]Jesus answered, "Truly, truly, I say to you, unless one is born of water and the Spirit, he cannot enter the kingdom of God. [6]That which is born of the flesh is flesh, and that which is born of the Spirit is spirit. [7]Do not marvel that I said to you, 'Youd must be born again.' [8]The winde blows where it wishes, and you hear its sound, but you do not know where it comes from or where it goes. So it is with everyone who is born of the Spirit." (ESV)

What is Spirit here, then? What is that word "Spirit" pointing at? Beyond there, we should try and establish what is "flesh" pointing at also?

I will start with flesh, and speak from all I have seen, explored, and reflected on in this change of who I am. Compared to the writings of others, the teachings of others, such as Yeshua/Jesus, then the flesh seems to reflect deeply the self, or at least the parts of self that derail us from our best path.

Self in and of its nature is ultimately in a state of wanting and longing. When we are in awareness, in the freedom of the "I am-ness" and acceptance of that, then we feel immense contentment. We feel whole, loved, and nourished. We feel a presence and unity with all things. It lightens our heart and gives us a break from the worries and anxieties of the self and its persistent need to control, take responsibility, and uphold this game of being led by language to believe it, knows where it is, and know what it is, whilst all the while knowing nothing.

When we are in self, we are not feeling that unity, wholeness, and oneness. We feel separated and often isolated, even when surrounded by so many.

That sense of separation the mind has created to help us function and ground into a life here. Not being offered an antidote, the antidote being reconnecting with awareness ultimately, leaves us wanting something, and that something is energy, which is frequency. It is our human condition. We are beings of wanting energy; the more energy we have, the better we feel.

The highest state of vibration and frequency for a human is found in the I am-ness, the unity. You can know this through directly sitting in it. You do not need to believe me when I say that it is so. It is a fact we can all explore. When that I am-ness, which is unity, is not there, we feel its lack. We want energy, a higher state or frequency. It is why drugs and porn are spreading so destructively throughout society. Humans search for that higher frequency through stimulation and pleasure. However, we are only vulnerable to such searches when we are lost in self and separated from awareness.

Remember John 1:1, "In the beginning was the word and the word was with God and is God . . ." All is vibration and frequency; science knows this too. It is all a unified field of atoms vibrating in different ways to make the different forms we see.

So, when consciousness and awareness become lost in self, the human can begin to want energy very badly. The more lost it gets from awareness and unity, the more energy it wants. Typically in the Bible, "flesh" references the part of us that seeks for its fulfilment in the world and not in the deeper unknown beyond.

Flesh and self are very much the same, that is if self is not with the I am. Self is largely a reactive, three-dimensional, on-sight way of living. We see the 3D realm, analyse it, figure it out, and move in the direction we evaluate as correct or most beneficial. Impulse and temptation of the five senses makes us follow the allures of the world over the voice of the compassionate guidance of the I am.

That is the man "born of flesh" that Jesus spoke of, the man of the womb. Flesh can behave well and purely, and work towards compassion and unity, but it can't do that without the Spirit that Jesus referenced at its foundation. That Spirit speaks once you have hung everything on the tree, as we did in the exercise in chapter two. However, if it speaks before, whatever is not on that tree will, in most instances, distort Spirit's voice.

Now what of a man born of Spirit? Spirit in the spiritual rebirth realm looks for something deeper, something more than what it can see. It lives for more than that also. It lives from a connection beyond analysis, the bustle of self made of thought, analysis, and memory. It lives for more than the eyes can see, for more than the mouth can taste. It lives for messages from an internal source, not reactivity to the external. In short, a man born of Spirit trusts something beyond the self for the movement of his or her life.

So, what is this word "Spirit" pointing at? We say it is a silent guide, immaterial, and not bound by any space or time. It is unseen, and yet it can manifest in the manners of a human's actions, intelligence, and self when renewed.

If self has been the dominant driver of life, analysing endlessly each day, then Spirit is the opposite. Is awakening to that awareness, the unity awareness that we dismantled into the I am-ness, the space where man can know the immaterial Spirit that Jesus spoke of?

How can we be born again? Christian or not, this process is important to see. The reason some Christians are born again and have light in their face, joy in their eyes, love to bring and share, while others have none, is simply this: the one who shines has been born of the Spirit, while the other has only added another label to the self that they are.

To be born again, in the regular sense of Christianity, is to agree to live your life by a certain set of moral codes and rules and to accept Jesus as your saviour, as a signpost for how life is to be lived, and to accept him as your teacher. This is a fantastic thing and brings a clear moral goal to the lives of many.

However, many spend a lifetime wrestling with the behaviours of self. They never quite leave self behind, so all of their corrupted nature remains: its bad habits, impulsive nature, and broken thought patterns. These people suffer. They are constantly feeling unworthy as they just can't seem to meet the standards expected of them.

They also may hold addictions, which are the uncontrollable activities of pleasure, activities that have been used to self-medicate through the trauma of losing sight of the I am.

I have seen such Christians go out into the world to love supernaturally, not because they feel it, but because the teacher said they should. It's not coming to them though, not naturally. They are forcing themselves to love as they should, and this too is an astonishing feat of faith and obedience to God's teachings, but it can quickly unravel even the best of humans. They are trying to match the unconditional love of Christ whilst living from the natural self. That self is the conditioner of love in the human story. It is the very reason we don't love unconditionally.

Love is beneath all thought. It is a potent energy known when we move from awareness to the stillness of the I am presence. It is there that love is known. Not the love of a person, thing, or place; rather, love that radiates from the human—love for the sake of love, pure love without direction or cause. This is the love that is the generous heart of God, the love that poured forth into all of creation and that we are part of.

That love is energizing, healing, and potent. It asks no questions. It casts out all of our fears. It is the simplest and most vibrant of all the loves on Earth, and it is only felt when self is not in control.

To go out in the world to love the unlovable, with self at the helm, is a quest I stand in awe of, but one that in most instances is going to bring great trials to the one doing it. For loving because you should is incomparable to loving because you do. Self will find reasons to love a person and not love another. Love that arises from Spirit, without self, will love all it meets in an instant. This deeply changes the activity and intelligence of the human.

Being born into that supernatural love, the love of Spirit, is about hanging those labels on the tree and accepting Spirit as the guiding light for your life.

For most, we adopt another label on the self, that of "born again." We have the imagery set, the words memorized. Yet, if we never went out and hung anything on the tree to make space for Spirit, then being born again becomes just another concept of self.

The struggle of following the life we should is tremendously difficult, as self is a low, separated frequency of consciousness. We want energy, and the world is happy to offer you it in all the wrong ways.

For most, the supernatural love of Christ is not necessarily born in their hearts, for they still feel separated from the I am, separated by the self and its labels, even if the self is not singing a religious tune.

Others, by some manner of surrender, have understood and let go of self, and they have allowed Spirit to take over. Spirit is our silent guide, silent but still louder than the world, despite its perceived, still, ever-present, penetrating silence.

I am aware I am a human. I am aware I am John. I am aware I am a Christian; I am aware I am born again. If I am aware, who is this one that is aware? When that awareness drives, we are undoubtedly far closer to God than before. The Spirit Jesus spoke of, that Spirit seems to be best known when the awareness becomes our priority.

Awareness is not structured in thought. Remember, only self is. So now life changes, it really changes, for the supernatural begins. You no longer live reliant on analysis and your intelligence. Instead, you live reliant on a different set of tools and paradigms entirely. You have the company of a cosmic intelligence, a guide of great love that speaks in the awareness, talks in the empty state, the I am-ness. This state of reduction, of self-free humility, is Spirit's presence having arrived in the human organism.

It is not so for all things, of course. Our analytical mind remains an important tool in life. If my car breaks, I can react with self, with its knowledge and know-how to fix the situation. However, I do so whilst fully aware of how close Spirit is to me. That Spirit is in me, through me, is me.

I feel immense joy, love, and compassion, which is why we must be born of Spirit; for if not, then joy, love, and compassion remain only ideas we should aspire towards, not energies we have been submerged in. Jesus said, "Take no thought for your life . . ." (Matthew 6:25). This space without analysis is surely the place whereby we can live in that way.

*B*ut seek ye first the kingdom of God, and his righteousness; and all these things shall be added unto you. (Matthew 6:33)

When self goes and awareness becomes the dominant state, we are automatically submerged in the love, the wholeness, and the joy of unity with God.

In John 10:30, we read, "For I and my Father are one, and I am saying to you, you too must be one as Jesus was.

If you are born of Spirit, you will be called sons of God (children of the Highest, Luke 6:35) This is something else Jesus said. Indeed, it is so. You will become a son or daughter of God, for now the awareness you are has overtaken the tiresome game of self.

*F*or all who are being led by the Spirit of God,
these are sons of God (Romans 8:14)

God is the great unknown. Awareness, the I am, is your connection to the great unknown. This "I am" is the acknowledgment of the great unknown moving in you. It is not an external force in the sky, but a force within you. In the words of Jesus from Luke 17:21, we learn,

*T*he kingdom of God is within you.

When pure awareness can look from your eyes—not self, no conditions on its love, no body impulses to avert its gaze—just pure awareness looking, doing, breathing . . . then by grace, you begin to see the world through the ever-loving eyes of God.

You may ask, "So if I can connect with awareness, as we did in chapter one; and if I stay there free of self, aware and humbled in my admittance of I am-ness, as we did in chapter two; then will that cosmic guide, love and light we point at with the term God, awaken in my life?"

I answer you, "Yes, it will, but only to the degree self is not present." For self can and will derail this whole process. Self can send you off to another spirit, not the one Jesus spoke of, but I'll cover that in the next chapter. For here we speak of a Christic rebirth, but there are other spirits, and you can just as easily, and unfortunately, be reborn into their catchment too if self is still making you misbehave, or having influence to make you misbehave, during this transformation of heart, mind, body, soul, and consciousness.

So when we sit in awareness, give up self, and trust that Spirit will transform our lives from awareness, how do we know what to do, where to go, and when Spirit talks?

This book is one of a series I am writing, so I will go into much more depth in a future book about our supernatural toolbox of Spirit and the gifts we have waiting for us there. This book is supposed to be about answering the question of how to be reborn, not telling you what will happen afterwards. For if you do it, you will know it for yourself. I could entertain you with supernatural anecdotes and stories just now, of which I have many. I won't, though. As for now, know that when we live from awareness, we live from faith, for awareness lacks analysis. Living from there will awaken the supernatural being you are, which is far more valuable than being entertained by the anecdotes of that state from others.

Your life begins to move blindly from the instructions found deep within your being. These instructions often don't make sense to the mind, and that's a good thing, for the mind is the natural. the natural is not bad; however, we have used the natural so much as humans that most of us have atrophied the supernatural.

You see the human in Spirit does not rely on analysis and self. It depends on something more. When this is depended upon, the Spirit and the human unite, and a new way of beingness arises. That human then interacts with the world in a totally new way. This way is far beyond ordinary understanding, rationality, reason, logic, and analysis. Now the cosmic intelligence of Spirit guides the human with synchronicity, dreams, intuitive capacities, visions, clairaudience, and clairsentience. The human, in short, becomes supernatural, which is exactly what Jesus said his followers would and should become:

*W*hoever believes in me will also do the works that I do;
and greater works than these will he do,
because I am going to the Father. (John 14:12)

Jesus did some pretty supernatural things in his life I am sure you will agree.

We no longer trust self alone, we walk to awaken the voice of the Spirit daily, which is the voice of God, the cosmic intelligence of the unity you are in, of, and from.

*F*or in him we live, and move, and have our being;
as certain also of your own poets have said,
For we are also his offspring (Acts 17:28).

Spirit is not sought with the self, for the arising of the voice of the Spirit in all its forms is mainly dependent on the self's absence. As an example to this issue of self shooing Spirit's voice from us, you might be sitting there and saying, "I want the Spirit in that stillness. Now what do I do to get still?" That voice belongs to self, and self is thought, and thought is the opposition to the stillness where Spirit speaks.

*B*e still and know that I am God (Psalm 46:10).

"A-ha!" you say, "I see. It the self. Self is the one asking. So how do I get rid of self?"

And there goes self again trying to control a process that the presence of self alone has caused.

Remember back to chapters one and two, and inquire into the voice wanting to do this for you, become aware of it, and understand that it is self. Then you, as in the soul awareness you are, can hopefully create some space again between awareness and self. Then anchor yourself in awareness and stay there. For when we stay there, Spirit's plans are revealed, that is once Spirit has taught us our new supernatural toolbox, and it will do so, I assure you.

Of course, that Spirit is God, and that voice and presence arising from the stillness we embrace when in I am-ness, that is grace. For notice you did not need to earn it, pursue it, or fulfil a law to have it. In fact, searching for it sends it away. For in searching, you engage the self and its analysis. From there you will fill up the human with self again rather than walking in awareness and Spirit. It is by grace you will know God, for you are loved right here, right now. The only blockage to that is that you are not born of Spirit yet, or perhaps your mind has told you that you are, while self has sneakily remained in the driving seat of your life.

The interesting thing is that the seeker initially needed guidance only from books and elders—advice and guidance on what is right and what is wrong, how to live, and how to be. For all these things are hugely beneficial and important.

Something new happens in us. When that state of consciousness, that presence of Spirit, and the elevated frequency it brings us is present, it radiates in our hearts. Then we develop a new conscience, a new sensitivity to the world. The joy, peace, and freedom when living from unity, from Spirit, from the I am-ness and all it has to reveal to us is so powerful that the former temptations of the world become meaningless to us. For if we indulge but once, we acknowledge that they lower us; we sense pain in our transgressions.

We know the place within us whereby other humans wrote the stories of love, compassion, corruption, and falling men. We know it. It is written in us now, and for all we can fall, it's a lot harder for the world to make it so, for we simply have too much to lose. Not the idea of it, or the fear of it, but to actually lose the pure heightened presence and joy of the I am, and the miraculous life, gifts, and provisions it reveals and leads us too.

The new human, the spirit man, the one born again, awakened from duality into unity—the reverse of Adam and Eve's fall from unity into duality—now has the cosmic love and intelligence, God, as the driver. That human will know the supernatural life and the difference between the natural one most of us were raised with compared to the new interactions and movements in and with reality that Spirit has opened to the human organism and the soul awareness animating it.

34

Chapter 5: Now, How Do We Live?

(Managed by Awareness)

*I*f you are not a monk living a monastic life, nor a hermit exploring consciousness deep in the forest, then the self is needed. We need to be fathers and mothers and employers and employees. We need to have these roles in making the magical workings of society function.

When we become aware of self, we become aware of the attributes of self, the names, roles, and labels that we use to create this image of who we are on top of this mystery of the I am-ness we are. Then we do not lose self; we only place the self down for a time.

We return to the unity, the colossal oneness of the I am, nourishing our hearts, minds, and souls with it. Upon a return to everyday life, the self will be there. However, what we should, and must, aim to do is to not get tangled up and lost in that self again. For if we do, we will lose the true peace, guidance, and unity of the I am in exchange for the idea of it, the memory of it. This is the situation many spiritual and religious people are in. They are a spiritual self or a religious self, but they have not an active connection to awareness.

The self and its architect, the mind, wants to be in control. Self will take any image it can. That is the nature of the technology of the mind. So just because you have an initial awakening—and you put down the birth certificate self, the nationality, the learned perceptions, the fears and worries of an old you—just because awareness arises and awakens, this does not mean that the technology that builds a self in you is gone. This is imperative to know.

For if the technology of the self is not understood, and if you do not understand how the mind forms an identity in separation, then the mind will create a new self out of the awakening. All the words, images, and information you have been drawn to will be enfolded into a new self, and this is at the cost of awareness.

When a human is reborn spiritually, this new being is living from the love of awareness: a new human. Now, however, if the mind grabs at that new rebirth and starts to try and take ownership of it in that human, the self returns, and catastrophe often awaits.

This tends to produce love and light on the lips, but not in the actions or way of being. The process is covert, but the development of a spiritual or religious identity can be as damaging as any other self. If a human was holding the self based in mainstream culture, and then has an awakening, and now absorbs new information on conspiracy, spirituality, practices, religion and the like, then this can be a good thing. But if the mind grabs at that and makes a new identity, and does so before spiritual maturity is achieved, then what develops is the frustrated con-spirituality of modern times. Though professing to love their fellow humans and wanting what's best for them, wanting to awaken them from the grasp of an unjust system and to them from oppressors, the one thinking and doing so is the same one hurling insults at others for being sheeple, the same one looking down on others as less than they because they do not think or do the the same. The self will form an identity and look down on others to elevate its fragile existence wherever it can.

Anything the spirit has helped a man master becomes an opportunity to look down on those who have not, not to pull them up, but to elevate the rampant self.

Those who do not master what is in this book and spin off searching for sacred knowledge will inevitably fall victim to this trap. They will yell insults at those who have not read what they have. They will put down those who live differently. They will de-viate from the love and unity of truth for the arrogant self who is hiding in songs of truth.

Staying rooted in awareness will keep the self humble. The man who believes he is more spiritual because he is celibate while another man has a family, is in an ego trap. The woman who believes she is more spiritual as she rides a bicycle while another drives a car is in an ego trap. Doing what is better for the environment does not earn you spiritual points.

Any idea, identity, or role you get caught on or caught in, thinking you are more spiritual, is undoubtedly the self posing as awakened.

When you understand this, you will understand why many re-ligions have failed. Many who awaken into unity fall into worldly behaviors. They have developed a new identity but are not living in spirit. The walk of rebirth is walked with awareness at its helm. When self and mind try to own that, a subtle but devastating ex-change takes place.

The human will swap out the presence of the I am for a memo-ry of the I am. It will swap out the presence, the love, and the peace of being of the I am Spirit in exchange for the descriptions, the im-ages, and the ideas that self conjures us to represent the I am.

The idea and memory of the generous heart guiding you is not the generous heart guiding you. The image that you are a sur-rendered servant of God is not the actuality of you being a surren-dered servant of God. The two are separate; one is humble, and one believes it is.

The self is full of pride. It is the birthplace of pride, in fact. The self is the soil in which pride takes root. Now you may have a human who walks in awareness, in the will of Spirit. He does well and he serves, and Spirit gifts the man anointings to make that path go smoothly. The anointing, the guidance, and the way were all from Spirit, all revealed and gifted when the self was not running the show. Then self steps in.

Self looks at the memories that the human driven by Spir-it created, and the technology of the mind that creates self says,

"Look what I did." Self begins to take credit for the work the Spirit has done. This work done through the human organism is work Spirit created to begin with. The self in separation likes to forget God. It overlooks the anointings from the generous heart, and it parades itself as the author of God's work, craving praise to stabilize its unstable, illusory nature.

Even if the self is singing the song of Spirit's work, using all the jargon and terms of spirituality and religion, quoting all the scriptures, and promoting all the spiritual or awakened activities, then that self is just as bad as any self, for it will still sit on the throne. It will still create a void from the unity with spirit. It will speak of unity and know it in memory, but unity's actual presence is lost to it. The self will come, it must come, but we must watch for it.

When the self builds the image of a spiritual self, the risks are somehow more serious, as its existence is somewhat covert. The self that is all about chasing worldly desires is clear to see, for it is obvious it has not overcome the ways of the world. However, when the self speaks of spirit yet is not of it, then it can be a very confusing time for those around it and the human it embodies. It speaks of love, but is not loving. It speaks of humility, but is not humble. It speaks of self-discipline, yet is not self-disciplined.

Sometimes this new self may pose as the knower of sacred knowledge, the guru of spiritual wisdom. When this happens, the character of self will play out the role. It will not point those listening inwards, towards the only truth that is the awareness, the I am-ness within. It will happily take the attention of others and continue to sing its spiritual songs while lacking an awakened connection, fueling itself from the memory of one that has long since been buried by the new self. This is an issue, as people who do this make others dependent on them. People go to such characters and surrender their decisionmaking to them; whereas, that character's aim, if adept, should be to awaken the guiding light of the I am in the community, not be the guiding light for them.

"For you should have no gods before me," as the Bible states in Exodus 20:3. There should be no person and no idol betwixt oneself and the I am.

The new self will be somewhat convincing that it is not posing but in actuality is the reborn. When this happens, we are often convinced by the thought veil, and self and will start to be lulled towards the world again. The void has started up again; you see, Spirit is not in the driving seat. That void is bait for the world's temptations, and the new spiritual identity that has created that void will start to wonder if the world has something to offer it after all—some sexual experience, material goods, perhaps a cookie in there it missed.

Yes, the return of self in a spiritual, conspiratorial, or religious framework that does not place God first is a trick the mind will play to get you back in chains to the world and that worldly self we all carry.

Other times the self will come more obviously, and the one who touched re-birth will run headfirst out of control into his or her vices, searching for one last taste of the world to know once and for all if they will leave it behind. This process is tiring, bothersome, and often destructive. The faster you can see through it and heal it, the better for all involved, especially you. This period sounds light-hearted and funny, but it can lead to disaster, especially if you have been in service to Spirit.

When Spirit works through a human, and if that human takes responsibility for it, aside from the arrogance of doing so, then the issue arises that the natural man and the natural rules now take responsibility for a supernatural work. The supernatural work can only be managed by awareness, not self; it can only be governed by the I am-ness, not the me-ness of self.

Self will inevitably become overwhelmed. For awareness knows God's presence in unity. It has no anxieties. It is in pure faith, and no belief is needed. This is a healthy, peaceful, and joyous state. The self that is living by the idea and memory of unity does not actually feel that peace. Therefore, it can feel increasingly anxious about the work, as it is taking responsibility for the work of Spirit.

The self also will start to take responsibility for the hows of Spirit's plans. Whereas in awareness the hows were taken care of by the peace and stillness of the I am and by prayer, now any tasks the human once moving in awareness had been managing as Spirit's extension—its surrendered vessel to the I am's will—will be done using the tools it knows, those of strategy and analysis. This change in approach puts immense strain on the organism. Instead of the peace and faith that Spirit provides to ensure its will is done, the self burns up the nervous system trying to solve things from a state of fight or flight, not rest and prayer.

No, a man cannot take on the work of God as his own. In short, the self of the natural man cannot manage the work of the Spirit—only awareness can. When the self builds a spiritual image and tries to command the spirit through carnal means, the results are always detrimental to the human.

The mechanism of self will always be with you, and it will always seek to establish a self-image that will be in competition with the will of God for your life. Where self is not, God's will is manifest.

Self will start with subtle notions that you do not need to worry about spending time in awareness It tells you that you are special now, and with all your spiritual knowledge, you are beyond that. Self will say you do not need to fast and pray as much; you have done these jobs for God, and indeed it is evident God is with you. Self says you do not need to be humble; you are serving the needy and promoting God's love, and that is sufficient because it is humble work. These are all stories of the arrogant self edging its way in, building a lovely new veil of separation, and one that is terribly hard to unpick, for it looks just like the awakened state did, only it is not it. It is a character of the mind playing out the role of it.

I share this with importance. Many spiritual gurus have gone there, and many have been hurt. I, too, as a man, went there and learned much from my spiritual self-image.

Just be aware, at all stages of the rebirth, that the mechanics of the mind that makeup self will always be ready to fire up and build a new self-image. So do not scrimp on the time you spend in presence or your practices that slow down self. Prioritize this time, even over the work God asks of you. Prioritize the I am-ness so that work is done through you, not owned or attempted by a spiritual image of self within you.

Chapter 6: How Do We Practice This?

(Preserve Your Energy)

A peculiar occurrence happens among a certain percentage of those who awaken to the unity and loving heart of the I am. That is, they fall into a not necessarily compassionate and empathetic space. They are reborn spiritually, but that rebirth takes place in a very different spirit to the one I am pointing at. The rebirth is born from a glimpse of unity, but the spirit of love, compassion, and empathy is not always the one that those who see this glimpse of unity end up walking with.

From all I have witnessed and experienced as this human organism typing this, there is a reason behind this. Our worldly activities have a bearing on our spiritual alignment and connections. There are specific spiritual laws in our reality that, when broken, have consequences on the heart and soul of a human. Awakening to the loving nature of God and seeing the world through God's loving eyes is a gift that always gives, but there is always a risk that the self and mind can contort, or be led to contort, the gifts of the Spirit.

Some awaken to the truth, the reality that all things have sprung forth from the loving heart of God, the truth that all things came to be from God, including the allowance of infinite potential and the gift of free will. To the spiritually immature, witnessing this in consciousness can be misunderstood to mean that all that springs forth from the field of creation gets the vote of a loving and compassionate spirit, but this is not the truth.

Infinite potential and free will are given, with trust that all will be used well and that the beings blessed with it will use it towards the alignment of the nature of the generous heart. They are given for one to align to a state that connects to the nature of the creation field, one of pouring forth love and creation, to for one to enjoy creation without misusing the energy field or those who walk with within it.

However, many take the gift of life and ignore the will of the generous heart. They seek their own five-sense stimulation and desires. They choose pleasure, endless pleasure. They choose the illusion of the world, the fallen world, over the Spirit that is their foundation. They want the sensory pleasure, and they want it now, now, now—often at any cost. You see, some are chained deeply to the world, to sexual immorality, lies, corruption, intoxication, and misuse of their fellow man to get ahead and gain access to these energies. They are chained to the world of selfish desires and ambitions.

When they have an experience of unity, falling into that unified field of rebirth and seeing the world through God's loving heart, they believe that because that heart allows it, it forgives, and it does not judge. The heart of the creation field they glimpsed is the final say. They believe from this experience that all is one, and therefore their behaviours in the world are all completely acceptable. Those who have the awakening glimpse of unity through drugs and substances can go this way more easily than those who glimpse it through a broken heart, say, or a spiritual discipline such as fasting, or a prolonged losing battle with self. Perhaps even the sheer gratitude of God's creation did it. Either way, those who reach it don't always come back with the right message, understanding, and disciplined heart.

To believe that all is from the generous heart of creation, and that all pleases the heart, is a deception. The reality is that just because the creation field of life generously gifted all potentials does not mean the compassionate mind of God gives the vote to all that pours from its generous heart.

The River's Course

Like a river, the human's life and energy flows strongly and follows a course. The will of Spirit is at its back, providing it an endless stream of water to make its flow robust, free, and filled with peace. The river has a course, and the will rewards it with the vibrancy of life for following it.

Now, suddenly, the river develops a self. That self says, "Instead of following the correct channel today, I want to watch pornography and have some pleasure." The self has chosen the rush of a short waterfall instead of taking the course by which the river is intended to flow. In the time of falling down the waterfall, the self receives the illusion of the ease of being in flow. However, with each tumble down these pleasure falls, the volume of water is diminished. It is using up the vitality gifted by the generous heart and the will of Spirit. It uses this vitality for selfish means, and much exuberance is lost.

Now its waters are less, and the river feels it. It knows its waters are less, and the journey is now arduous due to it. So, the river has taken its first pleasure fall. It feels harder to flow due to this, harder to be happy and whole. If the river acknowledges that this temporary hardship was created through its choice to traverse the waterfall of pleasure, it might stick this hardship out until it is back in the flow and its water volume has built up again.

However, as the river has a self, and the self wants ease, the whispers are heard, "Psst, hey, why suffer like this? Come here and take this waterfall. Remember how easy it felt while you were actually in the fall?"

The river remembers but is tricked. It does not recognize that it again will have less water after the fall and feel worse. Still, the river takes the perceived easy route and tumbles down a pleasure fall again. Water flows to the lowest point as it is the easiest course. Over time, it carves deep ruts as it plunges again and again.

The choice to return to the way of flow becomes more difficult, as it has lost more water from the second fall. It has an option: Brave it and return to the rightful course, although with lessened waters, a period of discomfort awaits. If the river takes that way, all is well, the ease of its restored vitality is at the end of that. However, if it takes another fall, out of following the whisperings or because of deep ruts now developed, it has an even more challenging path ahead.

Of course, this river is you. The waterfalls are the calls of the worldly self to use divine energy for temporary pleasure, to worship the five senses, not harness them with the divine spark to do the divine will. The plunges our like our attention going for the thrills. Over time, like water, our behaviour forms deep ruts that we call habits. We, too, will take the easiest path. We, too, will take the valleys of habit we carve, and over time, we carve deeper and deeper ruts of habit.

The Bible says, "For the wages of sin is death" (Romans 6:23). We have long since said this is a physical death, but I am not convinced it is. For when we retain our sacred temple energy, the temple of God is us. It is not somewhere on earth; it is wherever we are. When we protect that, with a life of meaning, self-control, and a choice to follow the will of Spirit, then we feel alive. I don't mean merely breathing and walking. We feel joyous, present, and wrapped in a natural stillness that makes the world's heaviness dissolve. We feel filled with light, and our hearts are full of that lightness. Life is a joy.

Once you have known that place, which as a child most have, and then you indulge in sin, worshipping the world and the five senses, then you feel dead. You use up your energy, and your mind becomes occupied, not with creation, love, compassion, and joy, but with constant searching and seeking to fill a pit with no bottom—the bottomless pit of human desire.

Why we are lured to the world, why the self is the place that takes us there, and why that even is, I will cover in a later book. Trying to know too much before you know how to manage self and awareness is not a good idea. For now, all we need to know is that the river, after noting its error, should have taken the initial way back to its original flow path. It should not take the quick rushes of the waterfalls, be they small or large, for they deplete its vital water and lead it away from the way with each tumble. We are the same, and we, for the most part, when operating from self, will choose the waterfalls of pleasure over the narrow and arduous way, which is the way of redemption. We do this because the self lacks real love, wisdom, and knowledge.

The Mark

So, let us now talk about sin for a moment. Sin is a word that, by now, many have unfortunately seen as from some dated non-liberal rule book that modern man has grown out of, but sin is not this. Sin is a cosmic spiritual law. The origin of the word *sin* is from the Greek word *Hamartia,* and in Hebrew the word *Hata*. Both words mean "to miss the mark." What mark is that, then? We must look further into this to find out.

That mark is well described as presence. What is presence? *Presence* we will define as Spirit's arrival with a man once he has let go of self, stood in awareness, and arrived at the I am-ness connection. There we awaken Spirit's voice. There we awaken its loving companionship as a driving, guiding light in our lives. Meeting the mark takes discipline, but this is the way we must live.

*B*ecause strait is the gate, and narrow is the way, which leadeth
unto life, and few there be that find it. (Matthew 7:14)

The presence of Spirit will be moving your intelligence, and when we are living at this mark, we feel something. That something is best described as wholeness. We feel whole, with a sense of completeness and unity, full of vitality. We feel at home and filled with a lightness of heart and youthful energy. When there, it is in fact hard to live, as the joy of being seems enough. We are in this secret place of human consciousness, not easily distracted by the world or the plays around us, for it feels as if we are rested in the very heart of God.

When we find the space in which sin is nonexistent, we find a clear unabashed connection to the pouring forth of the generous heart of God. The creation field is the heart's gift of life, of consciousness manifest. It is the life that emanates from its infinite and eternal source of energy, the zero that is not zero, the source of all, the unnameable divine, the I am of all I ams.

When we are not in the form of a separate self, we are not interfering with that generous heart of God. We do not refract its will, its presence in our lives. We do not condition its love. We do not label its ways. We do not play the game of pretending we are organizing and understanding that which the mind cannot. Presence can be understood, but not by mind, not by reason, not by analysis—presence cannot be understood by self. Presence can only by understood by you as awareness. It is by the I am-ness that understanding can happen.

We feel its energy. When not refracted by the mind, the energy moves in and through us. We feel its love moving in all our cells. We feel as if we are that love, taking form in a shape we have pointed at with the term "human."

When at the mark, we begin to return home, to do the will of the generous heart that we are from and indeed are. We do not challenge it with our desires, our analysis, our self formed in thought and memory, which is the mind. We join the outpouring and its infinite generous plan for us in the gift of life.

With infinite potential comes free will, and with free will comes the opportunity for sentient life to separate from that union, the chance to form a worldly self and ignore the will of the cosmic heart. We make the exchange of that will of Spirit, the guide that speaks in the peace and stillness of the I am-ness, for the will of self. This exchange, most often in the form of pride and arrogance, takes over the driving seat, leaving the compassion of Spirit and Unity to wait its turn. All that which leads us away from the mark is that which misses; that is sin.

Imagine you are building up the energy given by God to animate your life, and suddenly you have a memory that sex feels nice. You are not in a spontaneous love connection with your spouse; it is all from memory. You, of course, do not control your spontaneous thoughts, but you do control them if you explore them with your attention. Now, not only has the memory arisen, but an attractive half-naked person appears in an advert. Now you explore the memory with your attention, whilst you begin to explore the person from the advertisement with your imagination.

Before you know it, you have used some of your vitality. You have spent it on an impulse from the flesh and the memory of pleasure. There might need to be more than this dip in vitality just once to side-track you from the will of Spirit being spoken in your I am-ness. However, if you have the same memory the next day, you say to yourself, "Well, that felt good, and it did me no harm . . ." So you indulge again. Only this time, the vitality drops even further, for it did not have a chance to recover. Beyond that, you are now carving a rut in your brain that we call a habit.

The next day you no longer feel whole. You are not as light, your heart is not as open, and the presence of Spirit and Unity are not felt as potently as in days previous.

The whole cosmos around you has birthed you. The the solar system has planeted planets, the forests have forested forests, the humans have humaned humans, and you are its end product. All that energy pouring out of God's eternal supply manifests in you. Now due to a program in the mind we call self, you have begun to take all of that sacred life force, and you have started to take life, plant, and animal, you absorb the sun, drink water, and breathe the precious air. You indulge in the precious love of God and in the love of one another, and you hold it all in your magnificent sacred temple of God, your body. Then you choose to betray that whole process.

For it wished to flower, you were, you are, its flower. It wanted you to bloom, to flower in compassion, creation, and original acts of love and tenderness that only you can fulfill until the end. Yet you betray it. You say, "Forget the flowering. Forget the original manifestations of what I can be. I want pleasure, and I want it now, now, now."

You betray the whole process by allowing self and all its arrogance not only to miss the mark but also to drive so recklessly for so long that the mark is even forgotten. Some humans do not remember a mark is there, and their fate looks like an eternity of struggle and turmoil. They blindly, as the walking dead, seek to fill the void, and of course are still missing the mark. Yet, they do not know where the mark is any longer, or that it is there at all, nor do they anymore hear the awareness to guide them there. They are now a slave to the world and its false promises.

How do you solve this? If you solve it with awareness, you will initially be faced with difficulty as you restore yourself. However, beyond that, the mechanics are still there to make you repeat this, so how do we solve that?

The Counter-program

If you have gone off course or are repeatedly missing the mark, you are now moving into the habit of doing that. This is where repentance comes in. *Repentance* is a word that again is buried in people's minds with images of authoritarian conservatives. Still, it is more.

Repentance is a spiritual law and the physical programming of the mind and its habits. Repentance, from all I have known, has two levels to it. The first is more pronounced and practical, the counter-program.

The brain is like a computer. Daily, by your thoughts and behaviour, you are programming an automatic pathway for attention to flow. You are developing a habit, a program. Daily, you are draining your vitality in some unconscious activity. That lost energy leaves you feeling disconnected as your frequency is lowered. To make a change from a self-destructive addiction or habit, you need to offer a counter-program, a new program to stop this brain activity, this mind and memory, this self. If you are leaving it unchecked, then you are not offering a counter-program. However, this counter-program is the first element of repentance.

The second is that you knock back on the whispering to the river, which is your self, by humbling the self. It is the self and its lack of control. The Bible states this: "Because the carnal mind is enmity against God: for it is not subject to the law of God, neither indeed can be (Romans 8:7)." The mind that moves based on the self's analysis and perceptions is outside of God's law.

When you repent, you acknowledge that the self does not know it is mistaken or opposed to Spirit's direction for you. You are a part of its creation, you who are its son or daughter. You are knocking on the door of Spirit, saying from a convicted heart that self has taken you away from your will. You are asking Spirit to please let you back in.

Of course, Spirit does, always will, for Spirit forgives instantaneously. However, if you do not acknowledge the error, then self will continue to lead you to spend your sacred temple energies on the stimulus of the five senses in some way. Spirit waits for you to knock on the door, to admit self's folly, and to ask to re-join the frequency of the generous heart's will and flow for your life.

The Risk

Sin is a real issue. It is against spiritual law, and if you use the temple's energy in short-term pleasure and for self's will rather than the will that moves our intelligence from the I am-ness or Spirit, then you run a considerable risk: the risk of aligning with the wrong spirit.

The man who is indulging in spiritual practice, who finds his way to unity consciousness, is in many ways more vulnerable spiritually than the man who lives out his life as a self alone. For now, that man is elevating his frequency, moving his consciousness to a higher dimension, into the realms of the divine and demonic. There are kingdoms of awakening that lay beyond mind and self.

If we are elevating ourselves, as we should be, to commune with the Spirit, with the angelic, we must know that they cannot persistently lower themselves to the 3-D density. We must go to meet them. If you fast, you will know how light you feel as you are moving into a higher space in consciousness, communing with the higher dimensions where the great unknown has helpers, conscious

49

extensions of its loving heart and will.

However, if you come back down to the 3-D, to the day-to-day consciousness, and persist in sexual immorality—let's say you run around with multiple partners and you lie and coordinate to make it happen, or let's say you are addicted to pornography, which I believe is one of society's most significant forces of darkness at this time—if you do this and take the sacred energy and vitality you hold in the temple and spend it there, then the self in you has just begun to deviate from the plan Spirit has for your human organism. You are worshipping the world, pleasure, and the opposition of the flow of God's creation field for your life. You are saying no to its plan for you in exchange for some short-term stimulation of the senses.

If you elevate your consciousness, and your actions do not agree with the loving heart and its will, and instead agree with the self and separation, which has its own spirit, then that spirit, due to its nature of separation, is also left dealing with a void. The void a human finds when overdoing pleasure is the void that spirit holds. That spirit needs energy, and it will seek it from you, and you will provide it when you miss the mark too often.

This is why many people get into practices that elevate consciousness and have frightening experiences. Society has taught them worldly behaviors, ones that true I am-ness cannot abide. They had no idea they were breaching spiritual law at all. They elevate their consciousness and are met with beings that are not benevolent quite often, beings from a higher dimension that break spiritual law and also miss the mark. This can happen, but only if you betray the generous heart's plan for you.

I have seen this happen a lot in psychedelic and drug-induced altered states of consciousness, actually. I am not standing here opposed to psychedelics, or plant medicines. I have met people whose lives have been changed immensely for the positive from psychedelic experiences, some ending years of addiction in one night. However, today the issue is that we have become so material as a species that we cannot guarantee this positive outcome.

I've no doubt ancient cultures used plants to commune with God. Christianity has evidence for it also. However, they also had a dedicated prayer life. They were not hedonists taking a substance. They fasted, prayed, and sought God. Today, people with cultural morality, which is not always a great moral guide, can reach for a psychedelic, and they move to a spirit realm without any understanding of where and what they are doing. This is why some have their lives ruined there, and others have them illuminated. The prayer life, the heart and the activities that the human partakes in, makes all the difference. In the end, focus on the substances instead of on the way of life, and on consciousness that seeks righteousness, is not a wise road to take.

Beyond that, I have lived with Rastafarians in my life, and some are like family to me. I love them dearly and trust them immensely. As Bob Marley famously sang about, cannabis can help you find unity consciousness. Sadly, others who find unity consciousness that way have used it to justify the wrong path.

When these Rastafarians I knew got high, they saw God's heart and mistook that it was all okay because it was from God's heart. They used this state of consciousness to better their lives at the expense of others' well-being. Deception and lies from God's heart, so they thought, and it was all okay—this was the attitude I saw in these men. They all inevitably fell from unity into a self that was governed by the spirit of the world, with notions of unity and love, but not of compassion.

In that awakening where one justifies all things from God's heart as acceptable, one walks the path of Alastair Crowley, a man who has been called the "Wickedest Man in the World," and a "Master of Darkness." The spirit he connected with told him, " 'Do what thou wilt' shall be the whole of the Law."

Love can be deceptive, for love of hedonism will give you an empty box in exchange for one filled with meaning. Love of drugs will see you lost from your best abilities, and in Crowley's instance, die alone, hooked on heroin. Love can be deceptive when it is not governed by the presence of the morality of spirit, or the instructions were written by those who have known that spirit's presence at the very least.

Wait, what of Yeshua and sin? It is the most well-known relationship of sin in humanity's story at present. However, I will leave that for now, for the crucifixion is not as simple as many have made it to be and, indeed, such a discussion would require a book unto itself to cover its anatomical, metaphysical, astrological, and indeed historical roots. If I tried here, I feel it would distract from the simplicity of this message, pointing us to the peace of God's presence and the freedom to explore our spiritual life without the separation of ego tainting that exploration too heavily.

What matters here is this: Do not be deceived into the false awakening. All comes from the generous heart of God; that is true. Good and evil come from that creation field, but it is colossal, and just because it does, does not mean all here get the vote of God or the agreement of God's compassionate mind at work. God hopes for more from us. When compassion meets our intelligence, we know it is not pleasant to be hurt; therefore, we should we should not hurt others. We know God had hoped for more from us when giving us free will. Had we not had it, we would be shouting, "We could have been trusted with it!" Well, we were trusted with free will, and look where we are—we are navigating a world filled with the misuse of it.

The Disciplines

Once you have missed the mark, the arduous journey you must take is that of the disciplines: fasting, prayer, and temperance—time to be in thanks and union with the Spirit as the wasted vitality is restored. I will go further with these in the next chapter.

Spirit will comfort us in those dark nights as we journey back to Source, where we are living in Spirit's will. Our energy needs are profoundly met. We feel alive, vibrant, and light of heart. Life is a joy there, no constant searching and seeking for desires, for the joy pours from within. It is not added from the external, from the world.

If you are not in betrayal and you stay centered, you will find the angelic awaits you, not the opposite. If we choose awareness, and we choose to stay in awareness, then awareness will keep us.

This comes by means of the right use of the sacred energy you are—your vitality, love, and consciousness that follow the will of Spirit. There you are in the creation field, along with the I am's heart and its ever-giving presence in your being.

How do we know how close to Spirit we are? Well, first up, peace is a signpost, as the Bible denotes:

And the peace of God, which surpasses all understanding, will guard your hearts and your minds in Christ Jesus.
(Philippians 4:7, ESV)

How do we practically stay in that state then? Preserve your energy, for the way of life and being reveals for you in the I am. At least begin with that which others who have spoken to Spirit themselves left in written word for you to see.

Preserve your energy. Build it up, and do not spend it on the will of self and its wants, desires, and selfish ambitions. Preserve it. Live for the will beyond self. Live for the eternal, not the world, and you will know Spirit that is holy and true. There you will see the presence of God, the true awakening filled with a profound inexplicable love for the innocent baby and guilty murderer alike. Remember, you are allowed to love people you don't like or agree with, but if you love them first before all else, you stand a chance of healing them. The mark of a true rebirth will be that love.

Chapter 7: How Do We Stay in Awareness?

(Taking the Body Back from the World)

*N*ow here we are, awareness, connected in unity. You are aware of self; you are hopefully not entangled in all of self's ifs and buts and desperate clamberings to be, but peacefully free of self. Seeing the world without language, memory, mind, and knowledge. Partaking without labels, without analysis. Simply is-ness, united in the dance of the heart of God that is the creation field you read in, and I write in.

All is well. You have stumbled into the stillness that is not forced, the natural peace that we see humans' closest animal companions, dogs, guarding as they joyfully and worry-free share their loving presence with all they meet.

You are here; you are now. You are part of the eternal now that is God's creation. Peace reigns supreme. Your heart bursts with love, and your soul longs to make that love manifest, shared in the lives of those around you.

All you must do now is stay in the elevated natural stillness that has overtaken the body and mind. That natural, unforced inner stillness and silence that remains still even among the chaos of life in time. Stay there and commune with the cosmic heart you are part of; know its plans, its will for its child you are. It is all joy, all bliss, and that bliss Joseph Campbell famously told us to follow.

Yet among that stillness, especially in the early days, comes a little bony finger that wishes to jab you in the ribs and steal it away. That bony, unkempt finger belongs to your body, but it is not on your hand. If pointed at anatomically, it belongs to your hormonal systems, your body chemistry, and its good friend, your mind, memories, and self.

You see, initially, as you sit there in the utter delight of awareness and sheer joy of that naturally still mind, your body still carries with it memory. Those memories are like chains that chain you to the density of the worldly ways, chains that keep you hooked on the abuse of the pleasures of the world and your five senses.

You are not bathing in the stillness of the I am-ness, but the body. The body has addictions, habits, and memories that know nothing about this stillness.

Imagine sitting in the most blissful state, knowing God's presence in your heart, not as a story, an idea, or a memory, not as a potentiality or goal. You are in the almighty, loving, compassionate Creator and Source of All's blinding light, presence, and love. You are, at that moment, overcoming the world. You are becoming a human who lives for the will of the I am. Those humans are terrific humans indeed. They love all they meet without knowing a thing about the persons they meet. They move with the will and wisdom of God as the guiding voice of their actions. Their intelligence is activated only by that bedrock of immovable compassion. They are great beings in the making, living for more than self and its ways.

However, suddenly, after years of indulging in dopamine-induced stimulation states—from entertainment, drugs, junk foods, etc.— the body's hormonal system begins to call. Then the memory starts to fire as it recognizes that call. Before you know it, this poetic state of loving presence I just described, and you hopefully know, become lost under a thought. A thought started by the body's impulsive call for some junk food, say. Now the memory of eating it comes, and the attention goes to that memory. Now you are moving towards junk food, and before you know it, you are eating it, and not to satiate hunger, but to try and find externally what you can only find within.

The body's memories and addictions just sought to drag you back from the presence of the I am and into the over indulgence of the world again.

This is inevitable, which is why we must reclaim our bodies from the world. It begins with the body itself, then we move to the mind. If the body is hooked on entertainment, pornography, drugs, or substances, it has gotten used to a certain state of being. That state gives it certain hormones and chemicals, and the memory of this sense of pleasure creates an addictive habit within us.

Without that network of hormones firing, the body has forgotten how to feel great. It craves stimulus when it would be far better off with contentment. We need to reset that body chemistry, which is integral to knowing who you are. You can know your essential I am-ness, know the awareness you are in unity, but the body will challenge that state, especially after the way most of us have lived in the current times.

How do you reset those systems? Well, at this stage, it is as simple as abstinence. Any addict knows the longer you stay clean, the easier it gets. The longer you find the will to not pick up junk food, the less appealing it is. The more times the body and mind call you to binge-watch Netflix or watch porn, and you say no, the stronger your muscles will become. Yes, this stage is an inevitable discomfort, which can be offset with other more beneficial activities.

I used fasting, water-only fasting. It is, in my experience, the greatest of healers in our human story. If you are addicted to a substance, I am confident from memories I hold that fasting can sever that addiction for good.

Fasting is a state of absolute rest to allow the body to reset its hormonal systems. You must educate yourself on fasting safely and be responsible for that side of it. You swing the pendulum to the opposite side in a fast. All your addictions, bad habits, and repetitive hormonal patterns you are hooked on are reset.

It is not essential, but it speeds up the process and is a powerful tool for humans to use and grow familiar with. We should all be fasting in some way.

Jesus said, "This kind can come forth by nothing, but by prayer and fasting" (Mark 9:29, KJV). That kind comes in many spectrums, spirits among them, but your addictions are among them also. Life-long bad habits can be illuminated into destruction, with some time alone in fasting and communion with the I am.

If you do not fast, then merely remaining in abstinence is a path, just staying in the presence and saying no to the body's impulses and addictions can reset the body and strengthen your understanding or mind and will.

Either way, the endless streams of pleasure will need to stop, so the body can reset itself to be at peace and in line with your new natural stillness.

Now beyond the body's addictions are those of the mind. A mind is a machine of habit, and it will desperately try to bring the actions of the body into those habits.

We cannot choose what thoughts we think, but we can determine if we provide them without attention. Right now, most don't even try to master this or have any notion they can.

We may look at it this way. Imagine we see five lanes of traffic, and we can observe the cars coming and decide which vehicle we still stop and climb aboard. Those vehicles are thoughts, but most people don't watch them, so they frantically jump in every passing car, and as they do, they don't really make much progress, for they are constantly moving from vehicle to vehicle, thought to thought. This is the exhausting state many live in constantly.

Some of these thoughts can be pretty destructive with it, unfortunately, and we still give them our attention.

This is where meditation comes in. You might not even realize what thoughts you are hooked on. Many of us are addicted in mind and hormonally to the thoughts that give us anxiety and stress. The self can take many forms, but many have a self that is a victim. They have not forgiven the past. In doing so, they have created the image of self as a victim of that past. Here and now, those memories that hurt them are only memory. They can only hurt you again if you pay attention to that memory. Often, if a memory is traumatic, thinking of it gives us a rush of hormones that make us anxious and enter fight or flight mode. Those hormones become addictive, and we become addicted to the story of being a victim physically and mentally.

This is not to play down your trauma. I have trauma; I had many years ago believed I should take my own life to escape the victim self that kept replaying and making life an unbearable thing. It is, however, to say with clarity that your past can only hurt you if you think about it or use memory to create an image of self today. Right here, the story of you, and all its traumas, are just memories; let it be for a while. Just become aware of it, aware of the story, and in doing so, you will see you are the awareness that is not penetrated or moved by the story.

So we apply mindfulness, meditation, we take no thought for our life. For now, you need to sit as awareness and watch those vehicles coming, watch your thoughts coming. You can choose with love which to get into with your attention. You can see how it feels to climb into that particular thought, and if it feels awful, you know not to catch a lift with it again. Of course, the reality is that some of the thoughts that make you feel terrible have been so persistently present that you are deeply attached to them. You are addicted to them. You have gotten into them and given them your attention so often that you may even believe you are them.

You are not, however, and you may even grieve them as you no longer give them your attention. As you no longer feel the rush of stress hormones they gave you, like any addict gets from a drug, then you may grieve them, but only because they make up a self that is now passing. It is now healing. It is dying in the manner it is integrating into you. No longer are these memories, when observed, coming forth to torment you. Instead, they come forth with wisdom to allow you to live a better, happier, more compassionate and fulfilled life here and now.

This, of course, applies to other habits you are aware do not serve you. You can watch the thought coming that leads your attention to the activation of that habit, and in watching it come, you have a chance to take a breath, take a stand, and say no. To say, "This body belongs to the will of the I am, and this habit, this story of self, this addiction does not serve the path God's generous heart has for this human organism."

When you can see the thought coming and say no, you have mastered the art of resisting and disabling temptation. You may make mistakes, as we all will in times of strain and unconscious behaviour. However, you will see that the helpless autopilot of attention on thoughts arising is no more, and now the awareness, the natural stillness of the I am, a voice that seeks to manifest the best you, begins to take the body and mind back from the world.

Chapter 8: What Is It You Are?

(The Love You Are)

$\mathcal{U}$sing language to point at reality, to point at what we are, is cumbersome at best. Words for most can lead to a significant loss of life and vitality, in fact. Some say I love you so often that they have forgotten what the words are pointing at. When you say I love you to your children and your loved ones, those words are not it. The love you hold for them is being pointed at with those words. When we mistake love for the words "I love," then love loses its flavour, vigour, strength, and overall meaning.

The reality is the sense of this depth of union, longing, help-lessness, protectiveness, romance, tenderness, empathy, toler-ance, and more is an energy within us that is almost impossible to capture with words. Yet often we see it in a look as much as in words. You can see love in someone's eyes, in their mannerisms to-wards another. Love is not words, and reality is not words, but we do our best to point at this clumsy linear communication system of ours.

The issue is, what if our true nature is one without time? If it is without time, it will not be easy to point at with a linear language system that, by its very nature of having a beginning and an end, drags time into it.

60

Wait, didn't we establish our true nature as awareness and the unnameable I am-ness that is reduced to? Well, yes, but let us look at what I am-ness, by its awakening, manifests in the deeds, desires, actions, and intelligence of the blessed human who falls back to it.

You see, we are used to love being in boxes—the love of friendship, the love of self, the love of romance or of parent to child, etc. These loves are valuable and beautiful, but they are not without their conditions. You might say this is not so, that you love your child without condition. Yet if you investigate this, you will see there is a condition, and the condition is a relationship. You have spent time with your child, you have known your child throughout, and this has generated a great bond between you that is perfectly beautiful in its own way. A mother's love, a father's love is a gift in this world, but it is, no matter how you look at it, a conditional love. Based on memory and relationship. It is not an automatic love, which is why some men and women abandon their children. This unconditional love we believe we have is not automatic, nor is it without condition.

If you held unconditional love for your child, then you would hold it for the children in their school, down the street, and the children you meet at the supermarket. Your love for your child would be the same as that for children you have never met. No, no, no, that can't be right, yet I assure you it is.

There is indeed a love that is not personal—it is not owned by the self and the mind, and it is not restricted by time and memories. It is a love that has no conditions, which is purer than the unconditional love we have believed we feel. That love is a conditional love of relationship of such vastness and depth that it feels without condition, but it is not.

As a father, the writer has had this alarming moment whereby the love I held for my own children could not be defined and separated from my love for other children we were with—children I had never met even until that day. How can that be? Is that not a betrayal of the love between parent and child? Well, I am going to say no. For what is better? What is purer? To love your child without a condition, or to love them because they are yours and you have a relationship and memory with them? This is not to make the two compete, but to distinguish something about our true nature and love.

When we as humans can enter the state whereby we see the world without organizing it—no language, labels, scientific dissection, spiritual boxes, religious boxes, memories, and knowledge of any kind—trying to fragment and organize what we are seeing, there we enter a complete and total union with it. As humans in that state of consciousness, we are arguably at that point the personification of humility. Even our spiritual labels give up trying to box life, and we humbly acknowledge the unknowable nature of it all. To analyse and organize the world is to create an organizer inside of you. That, in turn, makes the organized outside of you. Separation has begun, and the fall of Eden is there. You just separated from the unity of the cosmic heart. So, we see it without all that.

We become a loving witness, pure awareness at the moment. Pure I am-ness, in a dance of expanding creation that can barely be boxed with names and labels. When we are there, when you reach there, what is it that remains? What is felt? What is known?

What we feel when there is pure and potent energy. This energy is not earned nor found in another, nor in a memory. It is not bought or sold. It is not held. If we ask but once, "How do I keep this?" then we engage the self and separate from it in an instant. This pure, potent energy is so bright that nothing in the world that comes towards it can shake, move, or take it from us.

This energy remains when all the seeking is over, when all the searching stops. All the efforts to control it, find it, or earn it are over. What remains is what we see in a newborn child's eyes. It is the light of stillness and silence.

That light arises when the silence is not of the world, the world can be as noisy as you like, and this silence remains. For this silence is the natural stillness of the light abiding in man. The man whose mind has given up all pretence of control and understanding and has gotten down behind the soul and let the soul let out a mighty roar of I don't know, but I know, even though I don't know, that I am! I am here, present, and alive, whatever that is. I don't understand it, I don't know what it is, but I am.

There, free in the depths of surrender, the light that rises in the human whose self and mind have taken a knee to the Creator, is love, the light of love—pure, directionless, bright, guiding, compassionate love.

That love has no place to go other than out in every direction. The human's eyes meet a glorious scene of nature, and love is known. The human's eyes meet the most decrepit lost addict, and love is known. The human's eyes meet a child who is their own, and the same passion is known as the love felt for the addict. This love does not ricochet inside the perceptions, memories, and conditions of self. It flows freely from its source into the manifestation of form in the human story. The human meets the homeless child, innocent and broken, and love is known, love is felt. The human meets the one who has murdered, who has lost that innocence, and before the mind can say a thing and judgments be made, that love is known and felt. That love is the most awesome force of transformation known to man, and it is in us, beneath the us we thought we were.

You have no doubt felt it, perhaps when your loved one said I do, perhaps when your child was born, whatever it may have been. Some moments were so powerful that the mind, the self, and all the toiling works of conditioning and controlling it went silent. The moment in the world was so powerful, so beautiful; it silenced the mind, and that love that you are, that love that is in you and behind all things, came forth and shone.

You have felt it, only you felt it as life circumstances overwhelmed the mind and self into taking a knee. The mind could not control or organize the beauty. It had no choice but to surrender for a while as you and this astonishing beauty before you were unified. We know these memories, these times of great love. We all know them.

Now I say this to you: You can know them even in hardship, adversity, and the presence of the many lost souls that wander this world in our human form. You can be that love, for you are that love. That love, when it is known and awoken, makes a man crumble. It makes a man weep on his knees, for this is the love that started it all. It is the love without separation, the love that is the I am. It is the pure presence of the generous heart of God pouring forth all creation, and it is present in you, as you, and from you in human shape and form.

If the veil of thought is gone, then you have come as close to it as you ever will in this body, most likely. For you have died, all you believed you were has died. Yet you remain, the real you, the loving witness, willing, able, and honoured to follow the song of this immense love buried beneath the self you thought you were.

Jesus said, "If you come to me but will not leave your family, you cannot be my follower. You must love me more than your father, mother, wife, children, brothers, and sisters—even more than your own life!" (Luke 14:26, ERV).

Indeed, this is it. It is not a competition nor a request to not love your children and family. On the contrary, it was to not put that love, that personal, conditioned, often memory-based love before the I am. For when the I am, the love we are, is first, then we become the best most loving fathers, mothers, sons, and daughters. For now, we can touch love without the condition of a relationship; we can give energy freely, as it is given to us freely. We can become sons and daughters of God, for we now know the love of God. A love we were, are, and always will be. So long as self is not, that love is. So long as that love is, stillness abounds. So long as that stillness abounds, that love, that great light born of our inner silence, will make men holy, pure, and true.

That love is our salvation, our hope, and indeed our goal as men and women, to make that love—the forgiving, healing, love without condition—manifest throughout the story of humanity forever more.

You are that love. You do not need to love anyone as you should. This notion of "should" is gone, replaced with a love that loves with the same ease as which your skin accepts a cold breeze. You need to become an opening in this world so that love can do its will and work in the shape and form you once mistook for your name, nationality, relationships, and memories alone.

You are that love that truth waits to reveal itself to you, and if a voice in your mind now says, "Yes, I feel it. I feel it. How do I keep it?" that's the voice that took it from you to begin with. That voice can't keep it, and it can't control it.

If that voice says, "Yes, I want it. I want it. Now what do I do?" That is that voice again getting in its way. God does not need that voice; the spirit waits for it to be gone for its love to be perfected in you.

You are that love, where self is not. This you, the true you, the loving witness beyond the many gardens of the mind knows this all too well. May these words remind you of this and bring the return of that loving witness into sight.

So here you are, a being our words have pointed at with the term "human." Your core nature, I am-ness, is something so immensely divine, and when found, brings you closer to God than you have ever been or ever will be.

Before you explore the mysteries of life, the divine, and the world we are in, may you first know solidly who you are. If not, you will get lost in self again, suffer in an endless stream of spiritual or otherwise identities, and lose the loving witness perhaps for a lifetime.

Stay here, for a time, rest with the peace that surpasses it all. Stay with your I am-ness and learn from this. Stay until you know how to rest there at will. For learning to rest there is to learn to rest in the heart, love, presence, guidance, light, comfort, and protection of God.

Not as an idea, not as a concept or belief, but in the same way you rest in the arms of a loved one, you can rest in the arms of the I am, which are the arms of an awesome, wondrous, compassionate, and eternally loving God. All glory be to the I am in us all and the I am in all else that joins us here in this epic dance of creation, compassion, love, and life.

Who is the one writing this book? I sit here, totally aware of my name. Aware of my nationality and relationship roles. I am aware of all these labels I would like to describe as this writer. So what do I say? Who is the writer? What label will do for the one writing, when all is said and done?

I am. Just as the one reading this, when all is hung on the tree, is I am also. We are the mystery manifest, and we must give thanks for that always. Walk in its wonder and breathe in awe at its sights every day. Just as we did in Eden.

May the great I am, be with you always, in that natural stillness beneath thought, where that still silence births a great light, and that light of silence is no doubt the love of Christ made manifest through us in our human story.

Epilogue: How Do We Anchor the New Man?

(Affirmations to Anchor the New You)

$\mathcal{Y}$ou have ultimately read the book, but I hope to use this space to pose a simple notion to you and provide a valuable tool God has led me to use for life with it.

If I were to ask you again to hang all your labels on that tree— name, job title, relationships, scientific labels, spiritual labels, and religious labels—if I had you do that and remind you that there is one here doing it, it is none of those labels. Yet it remains here, stable, persistent, and still. I ask, "Who is that one hanging those things on the tree . . . ?"

The answer: "I am . . ." These two words are also a mask to cover the truth that we are a point of awareness looking out from God's great unnameable loving dance.

You are label free, yet still there, looking, listening, and loving. Still there, no tags, no roles, yet still you are, and still I am.

This, I am state, it is undoubtedly virgin consciousness. There was one born of a virgin, and his qualities were second to none. Compassion, love, patience, and tolerance. Selflessness, generosity, and acceptance to name but a few.

If such a child is born from a virgin what sort of child can be born from the virgin consciousness of the I am-ness you have found?

There in that space, when you make a home in it, and you choose to be there daily, Spirit will speak to you, lead you, and illuminate your way. However, we are humans with it, and we will have to contend with the world, our minds, and memories as this happens. So we can assist this process consciously, and help us to anchor ourselves more deeply into the new life we are born into.

If you have awoken the I am, you have found a chance to be spiritually reborn. That rebirth will be from the humble truth of not knowing and the loving peace of the virgin consciousness of I am-ness.

Then I pose this notion: If we have lived a lifetime with a mind and memories programmed by the world, culture, and the spirit that moves in it, then those memories are still with you. They may even try to resurface, and before you know it, this virgin consciousness of I am-ness will be I am-ing its old self back into existence.

If you were an addict, the virgin consciousness, for all it is can provide the stillness where the voice of Spirit is heard. It can also listen to the voice of the mind. We do not want to pollute the hard work of reaching the I am with old memories that define us. If so, then before long, you will be building a self you don't want on the blank slate you found. "I am a drug addict" is a memory. Let us forget it and find a new I am. Let us bring forth images of what we want to be, not what the world told us we are and made us into before we knew our true power and self.

Before we start affirming, let us be sure to set our prayer to be our highest good in the eyes and plans of the I am. Let us begin to hear what that will look like for us based on each individual and unique soul.

As we do that, we can choose the I ams that align. For example, if you have been led to teach, then choose to say such as, "I am a patient and efficient teacher."

Let us tip the scales in our favor. Let us choose the I am affirmations to discard, those that we will be hanging on the tree next time. Let us also choose the I am affirmations that stay.

"I am John." Okay, that stays.

"I am a child of God. I am healthy. I am compassionate. I am tolerant. I am peace. I am love. I am loved. I am a human in whom God's voice comes. I am a follower of the spirit of truth. I am strong. I am my highest good. I am God's servant. I am humanity's servant. I am meek. I am."

Affirming who you are helps stop the world from telling you who you are. Affirming who you are stops the old memories of you from filling that space.

My advice here is for you to try to create what works for your heart and intuition, but nonetheless I will share a few of my favorites:

"I am loved by God."

"I am a servant of truth and honesty."

"I am living my highest good."

"I am obedient to Spirit's will."

"I am present in every moment."

"I am brave."

"I am kind."

"I am strong."

"I am healthy."

"I am reliable."

"I am a human I can be proud of."

"I am a human Jesus can be proud of."

"I am intelligent."

"I am patient."

"I am living for more than selfish ambition."

"I am a provider and protector for those weaker than I."

"I am grateful."

"I am a grateful man/woman."

"I am beautiful."

"I am forgiven."

"I am forgiveness."

"I am loving awareness."

"I am God's loyal servant."

"I am love's loyal servant."

"I am unconditioned love."

"I am loved, and I am love."

"I am living a holy life."

"I am living a pure life."

"I am grateful for it all."

"I am stronger than I know."

"I am loved by God, I am protected by God, I am guided by God, and I am illuminated by God."

"I am a healer."

"I am the loving witness . . ."

So, remember to affirm who you are, to line up with the path the voice of Spirit has revealed for you.

If you get lost and can't find that awareness, come to this page from time to time and follow one of my favorite affirmations to return to the truth:

I am the loving witness. I am the loving witness. I am the loving witness. I am the loving witness. I am the loving witness. I am the loving witness. I am the loving witness. I am the loving witness. I am the loving witness. I am the loving witness.I am the loving witness. I am the loving witness. I am the loving witness. I am the loving witness. I am the loving witness. I am the loving witness. I am the loving witness. I am the loving witness. I am the loving witness. I am the loving witness.I am the loving witness. I am the loving witness. I am the loving witness. I am the loving witness. I am the loving witness. I am the loving witness. I am the loving witness. I am the loving witness. I am the loving witness. I am the loving witness.I am the loving witness. I am the loving witness. I am the loving witness. I am the loving witness. I am the loving witness. I am the loving witness. I am the loving witness. I am the loving witness. I am the loving witness. I am the loving witness.I am the loving witness. I am the loving witness. I am the loving witness. I am the loving witness. I am the loving witness. I am the loving witness. I am the loving witness. I am the loving witness. I am the loving witness. . . .

I am that I am.

I am your loving brother.

Made in the USA
Columbia, SC
16 October 2024

44502621R00039